I0149102

Presented To:

_____

From:

_____

BOOKS BY SHELLY BENOIT HENDRICKS

You're Chronically Ill... So Now What?

Your Loved One Is Ill... So Now What?

Visit Reneweddaily.com for more information

You may also contact Shelly via email @
shelly@reneweddaily.com

HOPELESS

30 uplifting devotionals for the chronically ill who struggle with depression and despair

SHELLY BENOIT HENDRICKS

Medical Warning and Disclaimer

The information provided in this book is for educational purposes only. Information found within this book is general and cannot address your individual needs. This book is not meant to be used, nor should it be used, to diagnose or treat any medical condition. Before using any information found in this book you should consult with your own physician. For diagnosis or treatment of any medical problem, consult your own physician. The publisher and author are not responsible for any specific health or allergy needs that may require medical supervision and are not liable for any damages or negative consequences from any treatment, action, application or preparation, to any person reading or following the information in this book.

Scripture quotations are taken from the Holy Bible, New Living Translation, copyright ©1996, 2004, 2007, 2013 by Tyndale House Foundation. Used by permission of Tyndale House Publishers, Inc., Carol Stream, Illinois 60188. All rights reserved.

All rights reserved. No part of this publication may be reproduced, stored in a retrieval system, or transmitted, in any form or by any other means, electronic, mechanical photocopying, recording, or otherwise, without prior written permission from the publisher.

Copyright © 2015 Shelly Hendricks

Book and Cover design by Brian Hendricks
Cover photo © Dreamstime.com, Cray77 (Pencil)
Back Cover photo © Brian Hendricks (Shelly's Portrait)

Renewed Daily Publishing
3761 Newcastle Drive
Sulphur, LA 70663

ISBN-10: 0692586091
ISBN-13: 978-0692586099

CONTENTS

INTRODUCTION

I live with two rare neurological diseases. This is my sixth year dealing with disability. I know what you're facing. I understand how hard it is to keep going when you face the hard dark each and every day.

Grief and depression are unavoidable when your life gets flipped upside down this way. Feeling big and real feelings is nothing to be ashamed of, and you should know that you are not alone.

This book looks at the raw terror of chronic illness and bravely helps you to put one foot in front of the other. These devotionals are honest and real and hopeful, but not in a contrived way.

Are you ready to face this with your God and a friend? I'm right here with you, every step of the way.

Let's begin, shall we?

AT THE END OF YOUR ROPE

"Don't be afraid," he said, "for you are very precious to
God. Peace! Be encouraged! Be strong!" As he spoke
these words to me, I suddenly felt stronger and said
to him, "Please speak to me, my lord, for you
have strengthened me."
(Daniel 10:19, NLT)

I so feel your pain! I really do, on a gut level, and I have
been there, too. What you are saying in your heart and mind
could be my very words... they are the words I have thought,
sometimes spoken and written down before.

It is so easy to feel that our families would be better off
without us, because we feel so diminished by what our illness
has done to our physical form.

It is so easy to think that we cause more harm than good,
that we are a drain on those around us, dragging our illness with us wherever we go and adding burdens to every
situation.

It is so easy to be led to believe that we have no value, that
we are invisible, that no one would even notice if we ceased
to exist.

You are not wrong to look forward to the day when we
can walk into Jesus' arms; in fact, I'd like to run!! But, sweet
friend, it isn't time for that yet, for either of us. One day we
will indeed receive new bodies and be relieved of our pain
and suffering, aches and pains! Oh joyful day!! But that day
has not yet arrived.

I believe, because God has whispered to me in my darkest times, that we are not diminished. We are not invisible. We are not a burden! We are changed and changing. The process is painful, but God is still able to use us, especially in our families, whether blood or one of our choosing.

The hole that would be left by our absence would be devastating and impossible to overcome. Even if all we feel we are doing is existing, that existence is the answer to someone's prayer. Truly. The fact that you are here is what someone begs God for daily.

Just your presence, your breath, your smile, your voice. It's enough. It's all they desire in this world, is YOU.

There is so much more in store for you that the Lord longs to show you, in time, but I know that today is not the day for that discussion.

Today I just want you to hear these few things:

1. God Sees You, He hears You, He loves You.
2. You are beautiful to us here; we need you among us.
3. You are precious, and to someone (probably more than one someone) you are everything. Everything.

Please focus on these truths today. I know it's hard. I know, because I have most likely walked a path like you have.

I know some days seem impossible, truly un-do-able. But please remember that nothing is impossible with God. Let Him carry you through these times; lean on Him minute by minute.

And please, friend, please don't leave us.

Father,

I lift up the readers here today in a special and mighty way. Touch each one in the way that they most need. Allow them to feel Your presence in a tangible way today. Let them know that they are not alone and that they are very, very valuable.

In Jesus' Name, Amen...

LET'S GO DEEPER:

1. Have you thought that the world would be better off without you?

_____

_____

_____

_____

2. How did those things make you feel about yourself?

_____

_____

_____

_____

3. Write here a verse that helps you to remember that your life matters.

_____

_____

_____

_____

4. What is one thing you can do, today, to reach out for help?

_____

_____

_____

_____

HEDGE OF PROTECTION

But now, why have you broken down our wall so that all who pass by may steal our fruit? The wild boar from the forest devours it, and the wild animals feed on it.
(Psalm 80:12-13, NLT)

Depression. It's defined as a sunken place or part; an area lower than the surrounding surface.

I think that's a pretty accurate description of how the face of depression feels. But dig down below the surface and it won't take any time to find much stronger things.... things like despair, anger, hopelessness. And I don't mean like the cartoon woman on the commercial who just needs her balloon re-inflated. Depression is a dark place, a quagmire of awful. I know because I have been there, and am positive I'll be there again. Chronic illness is such a roller coaster, isn't it? And heaven knows that life brings other struggles, some that seem to come all at once, piling on us until we can't breathe from the weight.

During my latest bout with depression, I was so angry with God. I asked my husband one day (ahem, at the top of my lungs)....

"Where IS He?? Where is my hedge? Does He not recognize that I need His protection right now?" I was not trying to be irreverent.

Oh no, I was completely sincere in my question! I was needing to feel my God at that moment, to know why I couldn't... was He hiding His face from me?

And my husband drew a beautiful picture for me. He said, "Honey, we're at war. The angels are standing over you, covering you all they can, but even if they're shielding you with their very bodies, in the midst of a battle, the enemy will still get past it and land some blows. And some of those blows will seem life-threatening. Because that's how they're intended."

I could immediately picture myself curled in a ball on the floor, and the angel curved around me as I would to protect my own child. Taking the hits for me, shielding me as best he can while the battle rages on around us.

I burst into tears, and everything changed for me in that moment. Now I see things in a different light. The darkness still comes, and I'm sure it will continue to, because we're in a war. But God has not left me unprotected, and that makes all the difference.

Dear God,

Please keep me aware of this beautiful picture of Your care in the midst of this hard time. Thank You for my husband and His insight into Your love.

In Jesus' Name, Amen...

LET'S GO DEEPER:

1. Think back to a recent time when you have felt you were without protection.

_____

_____

_____

_____

2. Have you cried out to God about it?

_____

_____

_____

_____

3. Write here a verse that helps you to know how to pray during these desperate times.

_____

_____

_____

_____

4. What is one thing you can do, today, to express to God your need for His protection?

_____

_____

_____

_____

SILENCE IS GOLDEN

A truly wise person uses few words; a person with
understanding is even-tempered. Even fools are thought
wise when they keep silent; with their mouths shut,
they seem intelligent.
(Proverbs 17:27-28, NLT)

Silence can so often feel like a curse or a dismissal. In the
midst of our anguish, our deepest desire is to be answered, or
at least acknowledged. On those longing days, silence is cutting, silence is harsh, and silence can be deadly to our faith.

I found myself on the edge of that death recently, and God
showed me some pretty awesome truths during those most
recent longing days. The first thing He showed me is that
when the silence seems to be the most oppressive, the voice
that comes in to fill it is often our Enemy's voice. His voice
comes in dripping with rage. He speaks depression into our
minds, he tries his best to plant hopelessness in our hearts,
and he waters these with doubt.

To combat that voice, I opened my Bible to hear what the
Lord says into the silence. And there in those pages, I found
that silence is golden.

Guarding our tongues is spoken of time and time again in
scripture. From the earliest creation, till the last verse of the
Word, we are admonished to be still or silent. We are commanded to choose our words carefully. We are encouraged
to be patient.

This started a journey for me, and I discovered some interesting things about silence. Let's look at it together from a few
different viewpoints.

Imagine with me, if you will, those all-too frequent and lamented moments when a dear friend or a casual acquaintance who is at a loss for what the right thing to say to you might be, or perhaps genuinely feels that they have great advice for you, says something like, "you look great!" or "I know how that feels, I had a killer headache last night that I actually had to take aspirin for!" Breathe with me.

Now let's look at that situation from a different perspective. Imagine if, when you showed up at worship services after months of not being able to attend, someone just simply hugged your neck. No words, no comments on your appearance, no jokes about you still being among the living. Imagine that the next time someone inquired, "How are you?" you told the truth about how you are, and instead of trying to relate, the friend simply put an arm around you and gave you a squeeze, or patted your hand with a look that acknowledged your pain without showing pity. Ahhh. Calming isn't it?

Freeing. Bliss. You see, what we are so desperately wanting is just an ear. A friend who could just be there with us. A moment of truth without consequence. Silence can be free of judgment, silence has the power to heal deep wounds, silence mends fences and drops guards. Silence is golden.

Now let's go back into the first scenario. You've just heard well-intentioned words that unknowingly cut deep into your already bruised soul. How do you choose to handle that situation? How do you choose to answer that person? Do you lash out in frustration and sarcasm? Do you snap off a witty comeback as if you are entering a verbal battle? Do you go into an explanation that will lead to feelings of guilt and sorrow for the one who was perhaps reaching out to you in the only way they knew how?

May I humbly suggest silence?

Silence leaves room for mercy, and could perhaps make it easier for the speaker to rethink what just came out of their mouth and perhaps rephrase or retract without feeling shamed. Silence also allows room for us to mentally step back and contemplate what this person means to us, what frame of reference they have for our illness, and what heart the speaker had when he or she spoke those words. Silence extends grace to both the speaker and the listener. Silence is golden.

Finally, let's think about God's silence. You remember, the one that sometimes cuts so deeply, and caused such a crisis of faith... Sometimes, do you ever feel so battered by your illness and the noise of the world that you just need to recharge? What is the first thing you do at that point? For myself, often it is finding the quietest and darkest place that I can find.

Sometimes I want music, but not the blaring kind, not the frantic kind, and not the kind with words. I crave silence. It dawned on me that perhaps that is exactly what my Father in Heaven, knowing how to give good gifts to me, is imparting to me... and I in my ignorance am interpreting the silent place and darkened area as an abandonment instead of a perfect peace. So today I will choose to thank God for His silence. He allows me to moan and complain and question without interruption. He offers silence as a balm to my weary mind. He spreads His comforting quilt of quiet over me. Silence is golden.

Lord,

The fact that You allow us to come before You is a miracle. I bow before You today, asking that You forgive me for all of those moments when I listen to the lies of the Enemy, rather than the truth I know of You. Thank You for silence. Help me to practice these things I've learned about silence. And thank You for the rest You have given me in the quiet times.

In Jesus' name, Amen...

LET'S GO DEEPER:

1. Have you found yourself facing more silence than comforting words lately?

_____
_____
_____
_____

2. How has this affected your faith?

_____
_____
_____
_____

3. Write here a verse that reminds you of the comfort of silence.

_____
_____
_____
_____

4. What is one thing you can do, today, to embrace the silence as a gift instead of a curse?

_____
_____
_____
_____

WHEN NOTHING IS EVERYTHING

In the beginning God created the heavens and the earth.
The earth was formless and empty, and darkness covered
the deep waters. And the Spirit of God was
hovering over the surface of the waters.
(Genesis 1:1-2, NLT)

Some days are so discouraging, as all I can think of is all
the loss, all the pain, all the struggle.

All seems dark and vacuous. My life is formless and empty.
I am drowning in the waters that are much too deep for me
to navigate.

Oh, but the Spirit of God is hovering. I am not alone here
in this place.

And the canvas my life presents is not actually nothing. It's
absolutely everything, because my God is the most amazing
Artist.

He has an imagination that knows no bounds. He not only
creates, He names and gives purpose. And do you know the
only building blocks He requires? That I be empty.

I can have hope in this dim place that oozes despair. Hope
because I know what the next verse was... and what the next
verse in my life will be as well.

Then God said, "Let there be light," and there was light.
(Genesis 1:3, NLT)

Lord,

Continue to hover. Speak loudly into my darkest days, and create in me a glorious unfolding. I dare not even guess what beauty You will make next.

In Jesus' Name, Amen...

LET'S GO DEEPER:

1. Do you ever feel like you have nothing to offer to God?

_____
_____
_____
_____

2. How do those feelings affect your hope?

_____
_____
_____
_____

3. Write here a verse that helps you to remember that He can do great things in and through your life.

_____
_____
_____
_____

4. What is one thing you can do, today, to find some of the light He placed in you?

_____
_____
_____
_____

TURN IT AROUND

To all who mourn in Israel, he will give a crown of beauty
for ashes, a joyous blessing instead of mourning,
festive praise instead of despair. In their righteousness,
they will be like great oaks that the LORD has
planted for his own glory."
(Isaiah 61:3, NLT)

Today I challenge you to turn around the negatives in
your life with a writing exercise. Take each challenge that
you face in your life and write it out. This in itself can be
therapeutic.

Now consider each challenge and find a way that God
can meet that challenge and teach you something beautiful
through it. He uses what we often see as our weaknesses or
failures or downfalls to draw us closer to Him. Before trying
this, let's pray.

Father,

*We know that You love us and long to draw us deeper
into relationship with You. Please as we list our
challenges today, help us to use this opportunity to heal.
Bring to mind readily the ways that we can see Your care
in even these most challenging of obstacles. Help us to
know that we are never facing them alone.*

In Jesus' Name, Amen.....

HERE IS MY WRITING:

Lord help me to see
that in my tremors You will steady me
that in my shortness of breath
You will cause me to breathe with more purpose
that in my blindness
You have so much to show me
that in my bruising
You will make me whole
that in my dizziness
You will hold me upright
that in my pain
You will show me deeper places
that in my crippled walk
You will make my paths straighter
that in my weakness
You demonstrate Your power
that in my desperate pleas
You will hear my longing
that in this new walk
You will teach me
to serve You anew

Now It is Your Turn:

RESCUE

I have come as a light to shine in this dark world, so that all who put their trust in me will no longer remain in the dark.
(John 12:46, NLT)

Sometimes I like the dark. The quiet, the stillness, the lack of sensory input is soothing. For a bit. But it doesn't take long to take over, does it?

A moment of doubt, a short time of pity-partying, these things are normal as humans. Especially as hurting and aching and scared humans. And aren't we all?

But it always amazes me how quickly those brief forays into sadness or fear turn into setting up homestead.

I mean before I even unzip my suitcase, I look around to realize there's already pictures on the wall and a lock on the door and my pillow is there on the bed. Hey, doesn't that recliner look familiar? When exactly did I move in?

He's a sneaky one. You know who I mean. He's like that slick salesman who has ocean-front property in Arizona that's just perfect for me! Before I know it, I've signed on the dotted line. Has that ever happened to you?

But Jesus, He knew. He knew that this world is a dark one, ruled by the dark one. He knew all the tricks and the pitches and how susceptible we would be to them. He knew we wouldn't sense the danger till we were already locked in and committed.

Are you looking for a way out? Then tell that debt-holder that the debt has been paid. You are free and clear and you are leaving.

So Christ has truly set us free. Now make sure that you stay free, and don't get tied up again in slavery to the law.
(Galatians 5:1, NLT)

Step out into the light with me, won't you?

Jesus,

How can we ever repay You? We give You all of our praise, all of our trust, and all of our love.

In Jesus' Name, Amen...

LET'S GO DEEPER:

1. Have you found yourself trapped in despair lately?

_____

_____

_____

_____

2. How does this affect your praise?

_____

_____

_____

_____

3. Write here a verse that helps when you feel trapped in the dark.

_____

_____

_____

_____

4. What is one thing you can do, today, to begin to experience your freedom through Christ?

_____

_____

_____

_____

WHEN YOU WANT TO GIVE UP

Then Jesus was led by the Spirit into the wilderness
to be tempted there by the devil.
(Matthew 4:1, NLT)

Oh, the wilderness. I don't just wander there. It's my permanent home. I'm a nomad, moving my yurt with me as I do my best to travel from one oasis to the next. But oh, those oases are few and far between. I've found that most are mirages, kicked up in my mind by the searing heat and unrelenting loneliness of this desolate place.

Do you ever just want to give up? I do.

I mean, is it really worth it, this continuing? Sometimes it sure doesn't feel like it, does it?

It feels futile. A waste. Hopeless.

I firmly believe that we have most likely all been there. If you haven't been there, hold on, because it's coming.

It is hard, I mean impossibly hard, to live in pain... to know that healing will not come... to feel afraid and a burden to your loved ones. When you see the future looming in front of you, wonder how you've made it as far as you have in so much pain, and then see it only getting worse, it is only human to be ready for the way out. Of course giving up seems glimmery and golden in our darkest moments.

Jesus felt that way, too. He knew pain. He was lonely. He felt fear and experienced loss. Jesus was betrayed and ridiculed. He was as human as you are and He prayed for a way out.

Jesus knows the wilderness like the back of His hand. He was tempted by a being who wanted nothing more than His utter suffering and destruction. A being who lives to lie and delights in deceit. An enemy invested in the downfall of all things Good and Holy.

This is the reason we do not give up...

(are you ready for this?)

We do not give up because the devil never does. To give up is to allow him to win. Even a small victory for him is unacceptable.

We continue on because we, like Jesus, state the truths of scripture aloud to remind both the enemy and ourselves of reality not warped by his vileness.

Repeat after me:

We were not redeemed with futile. For you know that God paid a ransom to save you from the empty life you inherited from your ancestors. And it was not paid with mere gold or silver, which lose their value. It was the precious blood of Christ, the sinless, spotless Lamb of God.
(1 Peter 1:18-19, NLT)

No life touched by God is ever, ever wasted.

He redeems me from death and crowns me with love and tender mercies. - (Psalm 103:4, NLT)

In Christ, there is no such thing as hopeless.
Let us hold tightly without wavering to the hope we affirm, for God can be trusted to keep his promise.
(Hebrews 10:23, NLT)

And so we do not give up. The glimmery is a lie. It's a dark rabbit hole, that temptation to give up. Hold on, Dear One. Hold on with me.

That is why we never give up. Though our bodies are dying, our spirits are being renewed every day. For our present troubles are small and won't last very long. Yet they produce for us a glory that vastly outweighs them and will last forever! So we don't look at the troubles we can see now; rather, we fix our gaze on things that cannot be seen. For the things we see now will soon be gone, but the things we cannot see will last forever.

(2 Corinthians 4:16-18, NLT)

Heavenly Father,

Grant that we may always find our hope in You alone, and be convinced of the truth of Your Word rather than the tricky lies of the devil. Thank You for never giving up on us.

In Jesus' Name, Amen...

LET'S GO DEEPER:

1. Do you struggle with wanting to give up?

_____

_____

_____

_____

2. How does this affect your prayers?

_____

_____

_____

_____

3. Write here a verse that helps you to remember that God has a plan for you.

_____

_____

_____

_____

4. What is one thing you can do, today, to cling more strongly to this life?

_____

_____

_____

_____

LIFT YOUR HEAD

But you, O Lord, are a shield around me; you are my glory,
the one who holds my head high.
(Psalm 3:3, NLT)

There were days, not so long ago, when I could not physically lift up my head. Those days may come again. And sometimes don't we all have days when we feel that the weight of the world and our circumstances have beaten us down so much that we cannot emotionally lift our head? I know I have those days.

On those days, I feel hopeless. I feel defeated. I feel ashamed. Why? Because the things this world values are self-reliance, strength and independence.

I thank God those are not the things He values!

The Bible tells me that my Father values dependence on Him.

Then Jesus said, "Come to me, all of you who are weary and
carry heavy burdens, and I will give you rest.
(Matthew 11:28, NLT)

The scriptures assure me that His strength works best in my weakness.

Each time he said, "My grace is all you need.
My power works best in weakness." So now I am glad to
boast about my weaknesses, so that the power of
Christ can work through me.
(2 Corinthians 12:9, NLT)

Even our plans are not to be made without His guidance and direction.

Look here, you who say, "Today or tomorrow we are going to a certain town and will stay there a year. We will do business there and make a profit." How do you know what your life will be like tomorrow? Your life is like the morning fog—it's here a little while, then it's gone. What you ought to say is, "If the Lord wants us to, we will live and do this or that." Otherwise you are boasting about your own pretentious plans, and all such boasting is evil.
(James 4:13-16, NLT)

But you, O Lord, are a shield around me; you are my glory, the one who holds my head high.
(Psalm 3:3, NLT)

This scripture reassures me that I do not need to "dig deep" to find the strength within myself to lift my head on difficult days (physically or emotionally). Nor do I need to feel like a failure if I cannot muster the motivation to lift my head in those times.

The answer is simple. All I need to do is come to my Savior. Broken, tear-stained face, head bowed down. He will not roughly instruct me on how to lift my head. He will not berate me for failing to lift it myself. He will reach lovingly down with both nail-scarred hands, take my face between his palms, wipe away my tears, and gently and slowly lift up my head.

That's it. Will you allow Him to do the same for you?

Dear God,

Help me to remember that when I am strong, that strength comes from You. Let me come to You to draw from Your well of hope, victory and courage. Most of all I ask that on those days when I cannot lift my head, I remember that the reason is because I am not meant to rely on myself.

In Jesus' Name, Amen....

LET'S GO DEEPER:

1. What kind of things make it hard for you to lift your head today?

_____

_____

_____

_____

2. How does the world suggest that you find the strength?

_____

_____

_____

_____

3. Write here a verse that helps you to remember that God is who we should turn to for all strength.

_____

_____

_____

_____

4. What is one thing you can do, today, to surrender your physical battles to Jesus?

_____

_____

_____

_____

THE MORNING THAT MATTERS

The faithful love of the Lord never ends!
His mercies never cease.
Great is his faithfulness;
his mercies begin afresh each morning.
(Lamentations 3:22-23, NLT)

The above verse is one of such hope, isn't it? Mornings are new.

Do you know what I've found? I've found that sometimes mornings don't feel shiny and new. There's nothing fresh about waking up to the same old pain and distress each and every day.

But today, I found that the same Psalms that tell us this:

For his anger lasts only a moment,
but his favor lasts a lifetime!
Weeping may last through the night,
but joy comes with the morning.
(Psalm 30:5, NLT)

Is the same Psalms where we find this:

I get nothing but trouble all day long;
every morning brings me pain.
(Psalm 73:14, NLT)

Now that, I can relate to. Preach it.

So what do I do when I come up against a faith roadblock like this one? With the devil whispering in my ear about how much pain each day brings... about morning schmorning... about not trusting in the One who gave His Son for me, or the One who took the nails without a word.

These are the times, Dear One, when it's time to trust. It's time to renew our commitment, to remember why we have hope.

> Let me hear of your unfailing love each morning,
> for I am trusting you.
> Show me where to walk,
> for I give myself to you.
> (Psalm 143:8, NLT)

There is only one morning that matters. Only one dawn. May we keep our focus there.

> Because of that experience, we have even greater confidence in the message proclaimed by the prophets. You must pay close attention to what they wrote, for their words are like a lamp shining in a dark place—until the Day dawns, and Christ the Morning Star shines in your hearts.
> (2 Peter 1:19, NLT)

Dear God,

Thank You for always being with us, even when life feels like troubles and pain. The hope You offer blows my mind. Help us to focus; help us to remember.

In Jesus' Name, Amen...

LET'S GO DEEPER:

1. What is the hardest part of the day for you? Why?

_____

_____

_____

_____

2. Write here a verse that helps you to remember that the Lord is closer than ever during that time.

_____

_____

_____

_____

3. What is one thing you can do, today, to focus more on heaven?

_____

_____

_____

_____

THE BOTTOM OF THE BOAT

Suddenly, a fierce storm struck the lake, with waves
breaking into the boat. But Jesus was sleeping.
(Matthew 8:24, NLT)

The wind of frightening changes howls
sounding like the taunting laughter
of our enemy

The waves of pain and grief build
crashing and threatening to drown
all in the boat

And Jesus rests His head on a pillow
and enters the sweet oblivion of sleep

The rains of doubt and confusion keep falling
drenching to prove the futility
of our next breath

The cries of alarm ring out from my heart
words caught and wrenched away
to disappear into the dark of the wet sky

But one scream resounds, is not lost.

Jesus was sleeping at the back of the boat with his head on a cushion. The disciples woke him up, shouting, "Teacher, don't you care that we're going to drown?"
(Mark 4:38, NLT)

Sometimes while all of this rages around me... Rages... I am overwhelmed and scream the very same things into the wind that the disciples did in that boat that day.

How else are we to react when we're sailing along, expecting nothing than that we will safely reach the other side, and all of a sudden we are in dire straits? Who else could we look to than the One who sleeps through our terror?

See, I forget. I forget the same thing the disciples did.

When Jesus woke up, he rebuked the wind and the raging waves. Suddenly the storm stopped and all was calm. Then he asked them,

The disciples went and woke him up, shouting, "Master, Master, we're going to drown!"

When Jesus woke up, he rebuked the wind and the raging waves. Suddenly the storm stopped and all was calm. Then he asked them, "Where is your faith?"

The disciples were terrified and amazed. "Who is this man?" they asked each other. "When he gives a command, even the wind and waves obey him!"
(Luke 8:24-25, NLT)

I forget that it's not about the brutality of the wind. It's not about the breathtaking height of the waves. It's not even about the torrential downpour that is filling our boat.

It's all about Who is in the boat with us. The presence of Jesus.

The disciples were amazed. "Who is this man?" they asked. "Even the winds and waves obey him!" (Matthew 8:27, NLT)

Have you forgotten, too?

Lay your head on a cushion. I've saved you room here in the bottom of the boat. Close your eyes and just rest, Dear One. He's got this.

Dear Lord,

Thank You for including in Your Word all that we need to stand in Faith. Thank you for never letting us drown, for calming our fears, and for deliverance.

In Jesus' Name, Amen...

LET'S GO DEEPER:

1. What storm are you facing right now?

_____
_____
_____
_____

2. How does this affect your faith?

_____
_____
_____
_____

3. Write here a verse that helps you to remember that all things are subject to Christ's voice.

_____
_____
_____
_____

4. What is one thing you can do, today, to allow yourself to rest in the midst of the storm?

_____

_____

_____

_____

THE TRUTH

Jesus said to the people who believed in him, "You are truly my disciples if you remain faithful to my teachings. And you will know the truth, and the truth will set you free."
(John 8:31-32, NLT)

Okay, so I'm going to get real here. I'm going to get down and dirty and talk about something that people don't usually talk about in loud voices or crowded places. But it needs to be said. It needs to be heard.

Here it is:

Sometimes life seems so hard, I just want to walk off into the wilderness and let nature take me. Some days are filled with so much pain, I wonder if taking a handful of those pills instead of just the one prescribed would be a better prescription. There's other ways, there's other whispers that I hear... quick to suggest and insidious in their timing.

Am I the only one? Something tells me there's someone out there right now that needs to read this.

No matter what personal torment brought you to this place, no matter what momentary slip that allowed the enemy right into your most secret thoughts, no matter what agony you feel right in this moment will never be right again... please believe that you are not alone.

Please pick up the phone or open up the laptop or walk to your neighbors. Ask for help, hit send, go ahead and cry.

Because the truth is that the voice whispering those thoughts into your own mind, the one keeping you beat down inside your own heart, that's not a voice that is trustworthy. In fact, that voice only speaks enough of the truth to be able to twist it into something dark and slimy.

Here is the truth:

> The Lord will not reject his people;
> he will not abandon his special possession.
> (Psalm 94:14, NLT)

> Can anything ever separate us from Christ's love?
> Does it mean he no longer loves us if we have trouble or
> calamity, or are persecuted, or hungry, or destitute, or
> in danger, or threatened with death? (As the Scriptures
> say, "For your sake we are killed every day; we are being
> slaughtered like sheep.") No, despite all these things,
> overwhelming victory is ours through Christ, who loved us.
> (Romans 8:35-37, NLT)

> This High Priest of ours understands our weaknesses, for
> he faced all of the same testings we do, yet he did not sin.
> (Hebrews 4:15, NLT)

If you have no one else to turn to, please consider me. Please. Day or night, I will listen, pray, listen, pray, listen, and then pray some more.

I can't fix your situation, but then again, neither can you. Isn't that a relief? We have a direct line to the One who can.

And He will. He will.

Father God,

I come before You today on behalf of all the hurting out there. It's a good thing You are so powerful, Lord, because there's a lot of us. And we need You, desperately. Thank You for being here, always.

In Jesus' Name, Amen...

LET'S GO DEEPER:

1. What are some of the insidious plans the enemy whispers to you?

_____

_____

_____

_____

2. How tempting is it to follow those plans?

_____

_____

_____

_____

3. Write here a verse that helps you to remember the TRUTH.

_____

_____

_____

_____

4. What is one thing you can do, today, to put HELP in place for those moments yet to come?

_____

_____

_____

_____

LIFE IN VACUUM

The Lord took hold of me, and I was carried away by the Spirit of the Lord to a valley filled with bones. He led me all around among the bones that covered the valley floor. They were scattered everywhere across the ground and were completely dried out.

Then he asked me, "Son of man, can these bones become living people again?""O Sovereign Lord," I replied, "you alone know the answer to that." Then he said to me, "Speak a prophetic message to these bones and say, 'Dry bones, listen to the word of the

Lord! This is what the Sovereign Lord says: Look! I am going to put breath into you and make you live again! I will put flesh and muscles on you and cover you with skin. I will put breath into you, and you will come to life. Then you will know that I am the Lord.'"

So I spoke this message, just as he told me. Suddenly as I spoke, there was a rattling noise all across the valley. The bones of each body came together and attached themselves as complete skeletons. Then as I watched, muscles and flesh formed over the bones. Then skin formed to cover their bodies, but they still had no breath in them.

Then he said to me, "Speak a prophetic message to the winds, son of man. Speak a prophetic message and say, 'This is what the Sovereign Lord says: Come, O breath, from the four winds! Breathe into these dead bodies so they may live again.'"

So I spoke the message as he commanded me, and breath came into their bodies. They all came to life and stood up on their feet—a great army. Then he said to me, "Son of man, these bones represent the people of Israel. They are saying, 'We have become old, dry bones—all hope is gone. Our nation is finished.'

Therefore, prophesy to them and say, 'This is what the Sovereign Lord says: O my people, I will open your graves of exile and cause you to rise again. Then I will bring you back to the land of Israel. When this happens, O my people, you will know that I am the Lord. I will put my Spirit in you, and you will live again and return home to your own land. Then you will know that I, the Lord, have spoken, and I have done what I said. Yes, the Lord has spoken!'"
(Ezekiel 37:1-14, NLT)

Oh, this life can just take your breath away, can't it? And often not in a good way.

Pain steals our breath. Sucks the oxygen right out of the room. Fear ensures that it stays gone.

Sometimes our interactions with other people can suckerpunch the breath from our lungs. Disappointment and guilt and discouragement is suffocating.

It's like living in a vacuum. We have no chance at all. Game over.

But what a mighty God we serve! Could it get any worse than the situation we read about in Ezekiel?

Dry bones. Not just dead, not just decayed, not just game over. They had become dry bones because their hope was gone.

Been there?

There was nothing left to even work with here. Ah, but God... but God.

Dear Lord,

You are the Almighty. Let us never forget that absolutely nothing is impossible for You. Remind us that You can fill us with life and breath even here in this vacuum we live in.

In Jesus' Name, Amen...

LET'S GO DEEPER:

1. What is something you have stopped hoping for?

_____
_____
_____
_____

2. How does this story from Scripture put that hope into a new light?

_____
_____
_____
_____

3. Write here a verse that helps you to remember that God can do the impossible.

_____
_____
_____
_____

4. What is one thing you can do, today, to breath a little new life into your dry dreams?

_____
_____
_____
_____

RESTORED OR REDEEMED?

Yes, you came when I called; you told me, "Do not
fear."Lord, you are my lawyer! Plead my case!
For you have redeemed my life.
(Lamentations 3:57-58, NLT)

Sometimes my grief for what once was becomes so real and
so suffocating, it feels as if I will surely drown. These moments
come out of the blue. They catch me by surprise. They hit on
days when I feel that after all this time, I surely have it all
together, and have moved past this deep grieving stage. Do
you ever feel that way? What are we to do during these times
when all we want is our life back?

Lately God has been at work in my life, teaching me (or at
least giving it a valiant effort) that I am seeking restoration,
when I should be embracing redemption.

Due to the nature of my illness, I have had to accept the fact
that I will most likely never be restored to my former state of
health and ability. I know many of you face this same discouragement. And the devil, oh, he loves to get in there and pour
salt into that wound as often as I give him the chance!

When others are headed out to a fun-filled day while I
am left at home alone, I hear him shout into my mind all of
the memories of when I could go along. I hear him laugh at
my longing to go. I hear him snicker into the silence of my
loneliness.

And it grieves me. Anew.

When my family comes home to a house in the afternoon that has no smells of supper and cookies being prepared for their arrival, I feel Satan going for the salt again. He pours in feelings of worthlessness as a wife and mother. He pours in guilt that they have to "take up my slack". He sprinkles a little extra doubt about whether this is true illness, or simply laziness run amok.

And it shatters me. Again.

When another bill arrives to add to the pile of mounting medical expenses, I can sense the devil's glee. He pushes my family a little closer to the brink of financial disaster. He plops another heaping helping of guilt right on my plate. He stirs the worries that I've tried to quiet all week long.

And it buries me. Afresh.

Why, oh Lord? Why can't things go back to the way they were before?

Sometimes when we are in the midst of the stripping away and the overwhelming changes to our life, we don't realize that what needs to change is not our situation but our level of acceptance and our reaction to it. God isn't in the restoration business.

He's in the redemption business.

If I can cling to Him through these unbearable times, He wants to bring me to something new. He wants to make worthwhile, change for the better, help to overcome something detrimental, and free from what distresses or harms.

When others head out to a fun-filled day while I am left at home alone, I hear Him whisper into my heart hope of days when the activities will be things I can go along for. I hear Him promise to never leave my side, not for one second, that entire day. I hear Him speak His truth into my life all day long, ensuring that I am neither alone nor lonely.

And it comforts me. Anew.

When my family comes home to a house in the afternoon that has no smells of supper and cookies being prepared for their arrival, I feel Christ's reassurance that all my children and husband need is ME, that I am enough. He promises me that I am leaving no slack, and that my family loves me. He strengthens my conviction that tomorrow is another day, and my slow cooker may yet make those smells a reality again. He will give me the tools and the energy, when the time comes.

And it mends me. Again.

When another bill arrives to add to the pile of mounting medical expenses, I can sense God's peace. He will never allow us to fall over that brink, of financial disaster, or otherwise. He lovingly offers me a reminder of my care for my children, and how I wouldn't even bat an eye over their medical expenses. He gently places into my mind Matthew 6... do not worry, He says.

And it refreshes me. Anew.

No, this process is not easy, and I know I'll still have days that sneak up on me. I am human, after all. And we are in a spiritual war, so I'm sure the enemy who I just saw slinking away will be back to pounce on me soon.

But the fact is that even if I am never restored to my former abilities and health, my life will be redeemed just as my soul has been, if only I will trust God and let Him bring me through this instead of trying to get through it on my own.

Heavenly Father,

Your care for me astounds me. Please help me to never doubt that You are working a great work in me, despite my struggles. Help me to be able to let go of the old and to welcome the new.

In Jesus' Name, Amen...

LET'S GO DEEPER:

1. Have you been longing for restoration?

_____
_____
_____
_____

2. How would redemption be different?

_____
_____
_____
_____

3. Write here a verse that helps you to remember that God is in the redemption business.

_____
_____
_____
_____

4. What is one thing you can do, today, to begin to change those longings to ones of redemption, rather than restoration?

_____
_____
_____
_____

THIS YOU CAN COMPARE

That is why we never give up. Though our bodies are
dying, our spirits are being renewed every day. For our
present troubles are small and won't last very long. Yet they
produce for us a glory that vastly outweighs them and will
last forever! So we don't look at the troubles we can see
now; rather, we fix our gaze on things that cannot be seen.
For the things we see now will soon be gone, but the
things we cannot see will last forever.
(2 Corinthians 4:16-18, NLT)

Lord, help us always to compare
the weight of our temporary pain
with the weight of Your eternal glory.

Father, may we constantly compare
the heft of disability
with the heft of salvation.

God, let us never underestimate the comparison
of the burden of loneliness
to the company of angels.

Jesus, remind us of the comparison
of the load of rejection
to the adoption into Your holy family.

Savior, keep forefront in our minds the comparison
of the mass of our worries
to the limitlessness of our Sustainer.

Creator, thank You for encouraging us to compare
the gravity of our earthly circumstances
with the wonders You have promised to reveal.

Therefore, since we are surrounded by such a huge crowd
of witnesses to the life of faith, let us strip off every weight
that slows us down, especially the sin that so easily
trips us up. And let us run with endurance the race
God has set before us,
(Hebrews 12:1, NLT)

In Jesus' Name, Amen...

LET'S GO DEEPER:

1. What kind of troubles do you have?

_____

_____

_____

_____

2. How do they compare to God's promises?

_____

_____

_____

_____

3. Write here a verse that helps you to remember that God
is faithful.

_____

_____

_____

_____

4. What is one thing you can do, today, to help you focus more on the promises than the troubles?

_____

_____

_____

_____

LEAD ON, JESUS

"Teach these new disciples to obey all the commands I have
given you. And be sure of this: I am with you always,
even to the end of the age."
(Matthew 28:20, NLT)

I've had many times when I thought I had reached the last
of the "new" news in these past six years or so. The time I
realized I was actually ill. The time that I knew this was rare
and chronic. The point where I accepted that disability was
for, well... ever. The hearing of the words "Primary Lateral
Sclerosis".

At every stage, it was like Jesus was just sitting with me. He
had His elbows on His knees, just relaxed-like. I sat beside
Him, head in hands. I looked up, straightened my shoulders,
briskly wiped the tears away, and said, "Well, okay then. We're
here. You're with me. I can do this."

And then I just would sorta start to unpack. You know what
I mean? Get comfy. Decorate. Settle in. Cause I mean, this is
the new normal, right?

Yeah, it sucks. Yeah, I was mostly brought here kicking and
screaming, but there's nothing that will change it, so I may
as well settle in. With Jesus, of course.

That's when it usually hits me that Jesus is not participat-
ing in this home-making. I amble over to sit next to Him
again. He's still in exactly the same position He was in. He
hasn't even changed facial expression. He's patient like that.
Thankfully.

I sit down next to Him, and just enjoy the silence, the peace that only His presence can bring. But I'm determined to hop back up and get that suitcase emptied soon. I take a chance and look over at Him. I smile to reassure Him that I'm okay. Surely that's why He's still sitting here, right?

Jesus, He doesn't move a muscle, just looks over at me, kinda sideways. The look on His face is pure sympathy. Understanding. It chills me because I've seen that look before. I know exactly what it means.

See, we're not really at the place where Home is yet. We're just going a bit farther each time. A bit deeper. Together, always together. And He just sits quietly while I come to terms, such as it is. Get a better grip. Adjust.

Accept.

Then He says, oh so softly, "You ready?" I place my hand in His outstretched one. It's warm and strong and tender. And nail-scarred.

That's when I remember why this journey is okay. It's okay because He's walked it already. He never moves me on before I'm ready for the next part. His instincts are flawless. And His love.... oh that's just mindblowingly big and deep and wide and perfect.

Lead on, Jesus. I'm right behind You.

Father God,
Never stop leading. And may I never stop putting my hand in Yours and following. I love You.
In Jesus' Name, Amen...

LET'S GO DEEPER:

1. What kind of "new" news have you had to absorb lately?

_____

_____

_____

_____

2. How much do you long for it to be enough, already?

_____

_____

_____

_____

3. Write here a verse that helps you to remember that Jesus is walking this road with you.

_____

_____

_____

_____

4. What is one thing you can do, today, to be prepared for the next step, whatever that might be?

_____

_____

_____

_____

YOUR SMILE

You keep track of all my sorrows. You have collected all
my tears in your bottle. You have recorded each one
in your book.
(Psalm 56:8, NLT)

Oh, the hours upon hours of watching "Annie". My sister
and I dancing around the room, singing along. Sweet memories. And this was one of our favorites.... "uh, you're never
fully dressed, uh, you're never fully dressed"... I-O-D-E-N-T...
I O DENT. Ah, yes. Great song, right?

No offense to Annie, but while I enjoy this song and to some
degree can agree with the sentiment, this song can be detrimental to our mental health if we take it too much to heart.
I mean, some days it's just plain impossible to wear a smile.
And, any day, it's impossible to wear a smile at all times.

Well, I mean, if you're interested in being as honest with
your emotions as you are with your words. I think that's
important.

Now, don't get me wrong... I'm not talking about stewing
or brewing or pickling yourself in negative emotions. I'm not
talking about spreading the un-love or bringing down everyone around you.

But there are moments when some honest emotions with
our King and Creator are things of true beauty.

Tears that are offered up on the holy breath of a prayer, they
shine like jewels on our eyelashes. Anger that questions from

sincere reverence, it sends a fragrant cloud of incense. Pleas for help that completely believe in the hope they are resting in, they blossom like a field of delicate flowers.

The difference comes not only in the way these emotions are offered, but in the care with which they are received. God makes all our honest emotions things of beauty.

And the smile you offer through tears? The way you valiantly allow Him to lift your head when you are bowed under the weight of care that threatens to crush you? That right there. That is pure, unadulterated lovely.

And it couldn't please Him more.

Whatever it is you have to offer today, it is beautiful to Him. It is beautiful because of Him.

Offer it, unabashedly. Don't be scared off if it doesn't include a smile right away. That's an earthly expectation.

God wants the real you. He's not afraid. He's big enough to handle it. Bring it.

Honest approach to the throne brings honest healing. It's the only way. I'm approaching today. Will you join me?

Dear God,

Thank You for never expecting me to put on a show for You or be anything other than what I truly am. You are my King, and I praise You.

In Jesus' Name, Amen...

LET'S GO DEEPER:

1. What kind of hurt has your smile been hiding?

_____

_____

_____

_____

2. How does this affect your ability to be real with God?

_____

_____

_____

_____

3. Write here a verse that helps you to remember that God cares about the pain you feel.

_____

_____

_____

_____

4. What is one thing you can do, today, to stand beautifully honest and raw before God?

_____

_____

_____

_____

SINK OR SWIM

Those who live in the shelter of the Most High will find
rest in the shadow of the Almighty. This I declare about the
Lord: He alone is my refuge, my place of safety;
he is my God, and I trust him.
(Psalm 91:1-2, NLT)

This life. Sometimes it feels like I'm just treading water. You?

No matter how fit you are, you can only swim full-out for so long.

Stroke, Kick, Breathe, Repeat. Sharks are circling. Storm clouds are gathering. Waves are getting stronger and higher.

This rip-tide of chronic illness is merciless. Grabbing, grasping, pulling us down and under. How long can you hold your breath?

Sometimes, you're given the strength to keep swimming. Sometimes He throws you a lifeline or a preserver.

But some days. Ugh. Some days, you look around and you know that this is it. No one is coming. And you just can't handle anymore.

You just can't keep swimming. Not one. More. Minute.

These are the times, dear one, when the grace is the greatest. These are the times when our God shows off a little. See, the myth of "sink or swim" is just that... a myth. God has another option up His sleeve, and He knows just when to step in.

The waves may keep rising, but God enables us to crest with

each one instead of swallowing the ocean as it crashes over the top of us.

The tide keeps on pulling, but God lends us a peace that passes understanding, allowing us to lay back and trust instead of getting sucked under.

Sharks are still circling, but God sends dolphins to ring around us and drive back the enemy, keeping us safe until we can again fight for ourselves.

Do you know how He does this? He doesn't give us strength to kick harder. He doesn't grant us the energy to hold our breath for just a little longer. He doesn't send out the Coast Guard to scoop us out of the ocean and warm us again.

He simply gave us a body that could float. He did this way before we ever needed such a thing. He knew what was coming, and we're already made for it.

Stop struggling. Just lay back and rest. Let the very waters that threaten to drown you, turn instead into a support, as you rely on your Maker to give you the buoyancy you need.

Trust Him. You were made for this.

Dear God,

Please help me to take a deep breath and float in Your arms. Let the waters swirling threateningly around me not distract me from Your trustworthy care.

In Jesus' Name, Amen...

LET'S GO DEEPER:

1. What makes you feel like you're barely treading water lately?

_____

_____

_____

_____

2. How does this keep you from just breathing?

_____

_____

_____

_____

3. Write here a verse that helps you to remember that God can be trusted.

_____

_____

_____

_____

4. What is one thing you can do, today, to just lean back and leave the burden with God?

_____

_____

_____

_____

SCATTERED (PIECES #1)

But the believers who were scattered preached the Good
News about Jesus wherever they went.
(Acts 8:4, NLT)

This life, it sure feels broken doesn't it? I feel broken.

God's been teaching me some interesting things about what
He can do with broken pieces.

This first of the series, I want to talk about the pieces that
are scattered.

The terrible persecution faced by the early church was certainly painful. It was difficult. It was heartbreaking.

It broke up families. It shattered lives. It scattered
foundations.

Death and destruction, pain and fear, these things domi-
nated those times and those people. There's no doubt about
that.

But what else happened? God used these terrible things,
meant for ultimate harm, to fulfill the commission of bringing the Gospel to every nation.

You intended to harm me, but God intended it all for good.
He brought me to this position so I could save
the lives of many people.
(Genesis 50:20, NLT)

If you're feeling shattered today... shaken to the core... hunted
down and tormented...

I pray that you will remember what God can do with persecution and persecuted people.

The evil men thought they were killing the church by scattering the members, but in reality they were fulfilling the Word of God.

They were growing the very thing they tried to stifle.

May the same be said of your faith, when you come under attack. May the hands around your neck increase the spark in your eye.

May you stare down the accuser and cling ever more desperately to the Rock.

As the pieces of you are scattered, send them out with the Good News of Jesus. You, in your brokenness, are a part of this... such an important and vital part.

> "He will not crush the weakest reed
> or put out a flickering candle.
> Finally he will cause justice to be victorious.
> And his name will be the hope
> of all the world."
> (Matthew 12:20-21, NLT)

Dear Lord,

Continue to scatter us. Help us to stamp each piece that is lost to us with enough of Your name that it can produce fruit, wherever it goes.

In Jesus' Name, Amen...

LET'S GO DEEPER:

1. What makes you feel scattered today?

_____

_____

_____

_____

2. Have you ever contemplated how God can be served through that?

_____
_____
_____
_____

3. Write here a verse that helps you to remember that God uses the scattered.

_____
_____
_____
_____

4. What is one thing you can do, today, that will cause God's name to be glorified in your brokenness?

_____
_____
_____
_____

CLOSER (PIECES #2)

The Lord is close to the brokenhearted; he rescues
those whose spirits are crushed.
(Psalm 34:18, NLT)

Sometimes it feels like just the opposite, doesn't it? The more broken our hearts, the more alone we feel. The more crushed our spirits, the more distance there seems to be between us and help.

But let's soak in the truth of this scripture today.

Our brokenness, it beckons the Savior closer. He longs to scoop us up and soothe. He is close to the brokenhearted.

Our destruction, it's what triggers the rescue. He races to save and protect. He rescues those whose spirits are crushed.

Do you qualify? I know I do.

Lord Jesus,

Let my brokenness and my absolutely crushing circumstances draw us closer together. Thank You for Your tender and timely care.

In Jesus' Name, Amen...

LET'S GO DEEPER:

1. What makes you feel wounded today?

_____
_____
_____
_____

2. Have you ever contemplated how you can move closer to God through that?

_____

_____

_____

_____

3. Write here a verse that helps you to remember that God cares for the wounded.

_____

_____

_____

_____

4. What is one thing you can do, today, that will cause God's name to be glorified in your brokenness?

_____

_____

_____

_____

MOSAIC OF LIGHT (PIECES #3)

For God, who said, "Let there be light in the darkness," has
made this light shine in our hearts so we could know the
glory of God that is seen in the face of Jesus Christ.
We now have this light shining in our hearts, but we
ourselves are like fragile clay jars containing this great
treasure. This makes it clear that our great power
is from God, not from ourselves.
(2 Corinthians 4:6-7, NLT)

Shattered dreams
lay in pieces all around

Faded designs
only hinting at what could have been
what should have been

Enough is chipped away from the edges
that the pieces no longer align.

Uneven curves

Irreparable damage

Eggshell memories
with sharp edges that can wound and mar

Ah, but You are the Artist.

Seeing patterns where none exist
redeeming what is destroyed
reclaiming unworthy and ugly

Revisionary Regeneration

The only way
to create a mosaic of light
is to first destroy
the wholeness
that constructed the dark.

Father God,

Thank You for being the incredible artist that You are in my life. Thank You for taking my pieces and showcasing Your glory in such a humble and amazing way.

In Jesus' Name, Amen...

LET'S GO DEEPER:

1. What makes you feel the dark today?

_____

_____

_____

_____

2. Have you ever contemplated how your brokenness shines a light?

_____

_____

_____

_____

3. Write here a verse that helps you to remember that God is the perfect Artist.

_____

_____

_____

_____

4. What is one thing you can do, today, that will cause God's name to be glorified in your brokenness?

_____

_____

_____

_____

REMEMBRANCE (PIECES #4)

You are reasonable people. Decide for yourselves if what
I am saying is true. When we bless the cup at the Lord's
Table, aren't we sharing in the blood of Christ? And when
we break the bread, aren't we sharing in the body of Christ?
And though we are many, we all eat from one loaf of bread,
showing that we are one body.
(1 Corinthians 10:15-17, NLT)

He was broken, too. Did you remember? Sometimes I don't.
He was broken for me.

Each week, I break off a portion of the bread and I remember. This brokenness I feel, He feels it, too. It has a purpose.
Both the brokenness and the remembering.

And I never want to forget.

It makes it easier to remember, having a broken body of my
own. Each time I can't, I remember that He couldn't, up there
on that cross. Each time I feel a pain, I remember the blows
He suffered.

This brokenness I carry around, it's a blessing of sorts, isn't
it? A reminder.

Through suffering, our bodies continue to share in
the death of Jesus so that the life of Jesus may also be
seen in our bodies.
(2 Corinthians 4:10, NLT)

Heavenly Father,

May my broken body show the life of Jesus. And may I always remember.

In Jesus' Name, Amen...

LET'S GO DEEPER:

1. What makes you feel broken?

_____

_____

_____

_____

2. Have you ever compared that brokenness with what Jesus went through?

_____

_____

_____

_____

3. Write here a verse that helps you to remember that Jesus was broken, too.

_____

_____

_____

_____

4. What is one thing you can do, today, that will cause you to spend some time in remembrance?

_____

_____

_____

_____

BEING THE TEMPLE (PIECES #5)

By this time it was about noon, and darkness fell across
the whole land until three o'clock. The light from the sun
was gone. And suddenly, the curtain in the sanctuary of
the Temple was torn down the middle. Then Jesus shouted,
"Father, I entrust my spirit into your hands!"And
with those words he breathed his last.
(Luke 23:44-46, NLT)

The tearing was necessary, so that we could enter freely into
the Temple. So we could be the temple. Dwell in the very
presence of God.

The veil was as sweetly broken as His body. And was it worth
it?

But it was the Lord's good plan to crush him and cause
him grief. Yet when his life is made an offering for sin,
he will have many descendants. He will enjoy a long life,
and the Lord's good plan will prosper in his hands. When
he sees all that is accomplished by his anguish, he will
be satisfied. And because of his experience, my righteous
servant will make it possible for many to be counted
righteous, for he will bear all their sins. I will give him the
honors of a victorious soldier, because he exposed himself
to death. He was counted among the rebels. He bore the
sins of many and interceded for rebels.
(Isaiah 53:10-12, NLT)

When He sees what can be accomplished through my brokenness, will He be satisfied?

Will I?

I may have moments of doubt and fear, but I'll tell you this.

I surrender.

Almighty God,

Be satisfied in me. Help me to see beyond this moment of time, so that I may share in Your joy.

In Jesus' Name, Amen...

LET'S GO DEEPER:

1. What makes you feel torn today?

_____

_____

_____

_____

2. Have you ever considered how that tear makes you the temple?

_____

_____

_____

_____

3. Write here a verse that helps you to remember why the veil was torn.

_____

_____

_____

_____

4. What is one thing you can do, today, that will help you to be a temple in your broken body?

_____

_____

_____

_____

IT'S MORNING SOMEWHERE

The faithful love of the Lord never ends! His mercies never cease. Great is his faithfulness; his mercies begin afresh each morning. I say to myself, "The Lord is my inheritance; therefore, I will hope in him!"
(Lamentations 3:22-24, NLT)

Just the other day, I was chatting with my sweet friend, Beth. It was a rough day and Beth was encouraging me, like she always does.

Me: What a rough day it's been. (or something to that affect)
Beth: His mercies are new every morning.
Me: (with just a hint of sarcasm) Indeed they are. Is it morning yet?

Let me pause here before I hit you between the eyes with Beth's response. There's something you should know about her. She's the wife of a Hero serving in Afghanistan. I hope you'll keep both of them in your prayers.

So, Beth, do you know what she lays on me? Here it is:

Me: (with just a hint of sarcasm) Indeed they are. Is it morning yet?
Beth: It's morning in Afghanistan.

I'll give you a minute to soak that yumminess in... I know I needed several.

Are you having a rough day, dear one?

It's morning somewhere. His mercies are new.

Dear God,

I want to thank You for blessing me so richly with friends like Beth. Bless her in a special way today, and help her words to carry hope into the hearts of the many who will read this.

In Jesus' Name, Amen...

LET'S GO DEEPER:

1. What night are you facing lately?

_____
_____
_____
_____

2. How much do you long for morning?

_____
_____
_____
_____

3. Write here a verse that helps you to remember that God is merciful.

_____
_____
_____
_____

4. What is one thing you can do, today, to embrace the morning?

_____
_____
_____
_____

I AM STILL...

These trials will show that your faith is genuine. It is being
tested as fire tests and purifies gold—though your faith
is far more precious than mere gold. So when your faith
remains strong through many trials, it will bring you much
praise and glory and honor on the day when Jesus Christ
is revealed to the whole world.
(1 Peter 1:7, NLT)

It's so easy to forget who we are when we face such challenges as our failing health and our increasing pain every
day, isn't it?

Just the other day I was telling someone that I forget that I
am Wife or Mom. I forget that I am anything but IIH (Idio-
pathic Intracranial Hypertension) and PLS (primary Lateral
Sclerosis). I feel like I am only the Power Chair-Needing-Lady.
So I tweaked this created this poem template. It's for us. It's
for you. Even if you just keep it to yourself, at least I hope
today will help you to remember all that you are, and all that
you still are.

I Am Still...

I am more than my power chair; far beyond the walker and
the medicines lined up on the bureau.

I am the velvetiest rainy day.

I am the magnolia. The great old live oak whose long gone
limbs I remember as if they were my own.

I am playing the music too loud and laughing too often. I
carry on Della and Lucille. I am never meeting a stranger and

loving big and a hot spicy bowl of gumbo and potato salad.

I am a teacher and a traveler and Jesus Loves Me, This I Know. I am a writer and an encourager and a listener and a praying warrior.

I am Louisiana and all things Cajun, and am reaching for Heaven with every breath.

I am still the imaginative sprite who couldn't quite keep from talking to herself right out loud. I remain passionate and just a little insecure.

I add to picture albums and hope chests and sometimes even comfy quilts.

And God makes me hopeful and indestructible.

I matter. I am here. Still...

Here is the template to make your own:

I am more than _____ (an aide item in your home)

far beyond _____ and _____ (products or everyday items you wish you didn't need)

I am the _____ (something soft) _____ (your favorite smell)

I am the_____ (your favorite flower) The _____ (your favorite tree) whose long gone limbs I remember as if they were my own.

I am _____ and _____ (a family tradition and family trait). I carry on _____ ____and_____ (family members) I am _____and _____ (family habits) and _____.

(favorite food)

I am _____ and _____ (things you dreamed of as a child) and _____ _____ (a song or

saying you learned as a child) I am _____
_____ and _____ and
_____(newly found skill or gift) and
a _____ (something you feel
strongly about doing) warrior.

I'm from _____ (place of birth) and all things
_____ (family ancestry, nationality or place) _____
_____and am reaching for _____
(a dream destination)

I am still _____
_____ (a story about a your younger self) I remain
_____ and _____
_____(details about the who you are
inside) I add to _____ and
_____ and _____
_(description of family momentos, pictures or treasures)

And God makes me _____
and _____ (how you feel in
your strongest moment)

I matter. I am here. Still...

Heavenly Father,
Thank You for never tiring of reminding me that I have
value. Please remind each precious soul reading this.
In Jesus' Name, Amen...

HURTING? YOU SHOULD KNOW THIS

1: God cares. So deeply, our brains aren't complex enough to understand it. So constantly, He knows every hair, every tear, every sigh. He misses nothing. And He is never unaffected.

And if God cares so wonderfully for wildflowers that are here today and thrown into the fire tomorrow, he will certainly care for you. Why do you have so little faith? (Matthew 6:30, NLT)

Give all your worries and cares to God,
for he cares about you.
(1 Peter 5:7, NLT)

I look for someone to come and help me,
but no one gives me a passing thought!
No one will help me;
no one cares a bit what happens to me.
Then I pray to you, O Lord.
I say, "You are my place of refuge.
You are all I really want in life.
(Psalm 142:4-5, NLT)

2: You have permission to grieve. And all that entails... the anger, the mourning, the questioning, and the doubting.

Morning, noon, and night
I cry out in my distress,
and the Lord hears my voice.
(Psalm 55:17, NLT)

"Why are you frightened?" he asked. "Why are your hearts filled with doubt? Look at my hands. Look at my feet. You can see that it's really me. Touch me and make sure that I am not a ghost, because ghosts don't have bodies, as you see that I do."
(Luke 24:38, NLT)

Then Jesus said, "Come to me, all of you who are weary and carry heavy burdens, and I will give you rest."
(Matthew 11:28, NLT)

3: Your pain gives you a unique opportunity. You can comfort others who are suffering in a way that no one else can. You can give not only sympathy, but empathy.

Lord, you know the hopes of the helpless.
Surely you will hear their cries and comfort them.
(Psalm 10:17, NLT)

Is there any encouragement from belonging to Christ? Any comfort from his love? Any fellowship together in the Spirit? Are your hearts tender and compassionate? Then make me truly happy by agreeing wholeheartedly with each other, loving one another, and working together with one mind and purpose.
(Philippians 2:1-2, NLT)

All praise to God, the Father of our Lord Jesus Christ. God is our merciful Father and the source of all comfort. He comforts us in all our troubles so that we can comfort others. When they are troubled, we will be able to give them the same comfort God has given us. For the more we suffer for Christ, the more God will shower us with his comfort through Christ.
(2 Corinthians 1:3-5, NLT)

4: Trust is earned. Hasn't Christ earned yours? Hasn't God given enough for you to completely believe that He cares for you?

For this is how God loved the world: He gave his one and

only Son, so that everyone who believes in him will not
perish but have eternal life.
(John 3:16, NLT)

"Don't let your hearts be troubled. Trust in God, and trust
also in me. There is more than enough room in my Father's
home. If this were not so, would I have told you that I am
going to prepare a place for you? When everything is ready,
I will come and get you, so that you will always be
with me where I am."
(John 14:1-3, NLT)

So do not throw away this confident trust in the Lord.
Remember the great reward it brings you! Patient
endurance is what you need now, so that you will continue
to do God's will. Then you will receive all that
he has promised.
(Hebrews 10:35-36, NLT)

5: Better days are coming. Whether those days are here on
this earth or at home in Heaven, you can know that better
days are ahead. In God's perfect timing, He will grant you
refreshing times, relief, and newness in eternal life. Hold on,
Dear One.

That is why we never give up. Though our bodies are dying,
our spirits are being renewed every day.
(2 Corinthians 4:16, NLT)

For we know that all creation has been groaning as in the
pains of childbirth right up to the present time. And we
believers also groan, even though we have the Holy Spirit
within us as a foretaste of future glory, for we long for our
bodies to be released from sin and suffering. We, too, wait
with eager hope for the day when God will give us our full
rights as his adopted children, including the new bodies he
has promised us. We were given this hope when we were
saved. (If we already have something,
we don't need to hope for it.)
(Romans 8:22-24, NLT)

I heard a loud shout from the throne, saying, "Look, God's home is now among his people! He will live with them, and they will be his people. God himself will be with them. He will wipe every tear from their eyes, and there will be no more death or sorrow or crying or pain. All these things are gone forever."And the one sitting on the throne said, "Look, I am making everything new!" And then he said to me, "Write this down, for what I tell you is trustworthy and true."
(Revelation 21:3-5, NLT)

Heavenly Father,

Place the truth of Your words and promises deep into the hearts of each person reading this today. Thank You for Your constant comfort.

In Jesus' Name, Amen...

LET'S GO DEEPER:

1. What hurts do you have yet to face?

_____
_____
_____
_____

2. How do those hurts block your faith?

_____
_____
_____
_____

3. Write here a verse that helps you to remember that God loves you.

_____
_____
_____
_____

4. What is one thing you can do, today, to replace your hurts with scriptural truths?

_____

_____

_____

_____

THE COTTONWOOD

"Even a tree has more hope! If it is cut down, it will sprout again and grow new branches.
(Job 14:7, NLT)

There are many analogies in the Bible that compare us to trees.

They are like trees planted along a riverbank, with roots that reach deep into the water. Such trees are not bothered by the heat or worried by long months of drought. Their leaves stay green, and they never stop producing fruit.
(Jeremiah 17:8, NLT)

When I was living in the desert areas, my favorite tree was the cottonwood. A cottonwood tree is always a good sign that a water source is nearby. In fact, they love to line the rivers and streams that wind their way through the rocky soil. They provide an oasis of cool and a pop of green in a dusty, red land. They tower above other trees, and send their branches skewing out in all directions to provide the most shade possible.

I can relate to the cottonwood. They have large, gnarly trunks that can withstand eroding sand blown by fierce winds. They have ingenious seeds that look like cotton and float lazily on a seemingly non-existent breeze. Their leaves are small but have a broad foundation and give the appearance of dancing with joy.

And there's one more way I resemble a cottonwood tree. But we'll get to that.

There's such a thing as erosion. There's such a thing as refining. There's such a thing as scars.

And then there's grief. Grief is a whole other animal.

Job understood grief. He grieved the loss of loved ones, he grieved the loss of safety and comfort, he grieved the loss of control, and finally he grieved the loss of his health.

Job knew grief. He mourned.

His tree was not battered, bent, broken, or scarred. It was chopped down. Destroyed.

Sometimes I hear that mournful "Tiimmmbbbbeeeerrrrrr!" wailed into my own life. My tree, my beautiful Cottonwood that shades the bend in the desert stream is destroyed. Utterly felled.

But here's the other thing you need to know about a cottonwood tree.

It will regrow. Re. Grow.

From a barren stump, while the tree itself lies decaying nearby, it will regrow. The roots of the cottonwood will access the stump as food, and send up tender shoots to find the sun. These shoots will harden and grow and will soon be able to feed the roots. They will grow to surround the stump protectively, or maybe rise right from the center to give it new life.

What Job knew is that the roots are the key.

So even on the days when the grief seems to cut me off at the knees. Even when that wail is heard in my forest. Even at the times that I have no choice but to fall at the cutting ax of grief and loss... I will regrow.

For my roots go deep and spread wide. I am planted by the river of living water, a source that will never leave me dry. My foundation is the Chief Cornerstone, and my leaves will dance again.

Father,

Bring me safely through these times of grief and destruction. Guide me through the pain so that I may

send up tender shoots again.
In Jesus' Name, Amen...

_____
_____
_____
_____

LET'S GO DEEPER:

_____
_____
_____
_____

1. What parts of your life does it feel have been cut off forever?

_____
_____
_____
_____

2. Do you believe they can grow back?

3. Write here a verse that helps you to remember that God

_____
_____
_____
_____

can bring the dead to life.

4. What is one thing you can do, today, to begin to regrow those tender shoots?

THE SETTING ASIDE

You must have the same attitude that Christ Jesus had.
Though he was God, he did not think of equality with God
as something to cling to. Instead, he gave up his divine
privileges; he took the humble position of a slave and was
born as a human being. When he appeared in human
form, he humbled himself in obedience to God and died a
criminal's death on a cross. Therefore, God elevated him to
the place of highest honor and gave him the name above all
other names, that at the name of Jesus every knee should
bow, in heaven and on earth and under the earth, and every
tongue declare that Jesus Christ is Lord,
to the glory of God the Father.
(Philippians 2:5-11, NLT)

Jesus set aside heaven. Divine privileges. Unimaginable power. Deity.

He shrugged it off. For you. It was the plan all along.

Christ did this for us, and God sent His son, so that He could pick up the mantle of humanity, suffering, weakness, scorn, and a cruel end. He bore the sins of the entire world, the entire history of the world.

He was willing to give this unimaginable mercy and grace because He knew that a greater plan would unfold. A greater dream could begin once He accepted this suffering. It was the only way for eternity to be shared, and oh, He wanted that more than He wanted to be God.

He wanted the chance to be with me more than He wanted to be the Lord of Heaven's Armies. He wanted you more than

He wanted to be the King of kings.

What have you, in your hardship, been asked to set aside? Dreams? Future plans? Goals you were working hard to attain?

Dear friends, our lives may have been rerouted... detoured... but I can promise you that God will never ask us to lay down a plan unless He has a better one. We will never be expected to set aside our dreams unless God offers a sweeter one. Any goals that are left to crumble will be the foundation of amazing new things that only God could offer.

Jesus trusted. He trusted the Father enough to set aside equality with God. He walked through unfathomable suffering along the way. As those nails were driven deep, I wonder if Christ had a question about if this was really, truly worth it.

When He cried out, "My God, why have you forsaken me?", can you imagine the anguish that swamped His spirit?

But God's plan was better. His dreams were sweeter. The rubble of Christ's earthly life and miserable death were the foundation that became the solid rock of the Lord's church.

How can we be expected to know, in the midst of our darkness, that the pain of these losses will be redeemed? Because God, who cannot lie, has promised it.

"And now I entrust you to God and the message of
his grace that is able to build you up and give you an
inheritance with all those he has set apart for himself."
(Acts 20:32, NLT)

We are entrusted treasures to the Great I AM. He is able. He has an inheritance prepared for us.

Let's be willing to set ourselves aside and put on Christ. We may share in His sufferings. We will have tribulations. But He has overcome. And He will deliver.

Since you have been raised to new life with Christ, set your sights on the realities of heaven, where Christ sits in the place of honor at God's right hand. Think about the things of heaven, not the things of earth. For you died to this life, and your real life is hidden with Christ in God.
(Colossians 3:1-3, NLT)

Dear God,

Please keep us grounded in Your word. Always.

In Jesus' Name, Amen...

LET'S GO DEEPER:

1. What parts of your life have you had to set aside?

_____
_____
_____
_____

2. Has this felt unfair?

_____
_____
_____
_____

3. Write here a verse that helps you to remember that God will bring you greater joys.

_____
_____
_____
_____

4. What is one thing you can do, today, to begin a life of true surrender?

_____
_____
_____
_____

THE WALL

A friend is always loyal, and a brother is born
to help in time of need.
(Proverbs 17:17, NLT)

Today I've been thinking about walls. I think before I became sick, I was pretty wall-less. I was just an open field and never thought about protection or defense.

There are many things that can come into a life, out of nowhere, and change it forever. Mine just happens to be chronic illness and disability. Maybe yours is grief, or depression, or addiction, or divorce? Whatever your battle, I know you'll know what I mean when I say:

The time had come to build a wall.

It was purely out of desperation. Truly, there was no forethought or planning... just a wild stacking of anything halfway solid, and a need to cower behind it.

I knew there was no way I could stand the losses. No way I could bear the disappointments and the grief. The arrows flying at me were flaming and sharp, and they were aimed with wicked marksmanship.

Some were intentional, and some were just ignorantly let loose. I think those hurt the most. I mean, we expect arrows from enemies, right? Not so much the friendly fire. That's always more tragic.

That's when I began to use tears to mix my mortar... I had to strengthen the cracks in my wall. The ones the let in drafts and whispers and sometimes spirits that meant nothing but harm.

I retreated. Living in the dark, scrounging what I could, splitting into a double mind and cowering before the blows could even come. Living life on all-fours for so long that I forgot what it was to stand tall. Forgot what it was to receive a kindness. Forgot what it was to share a hope.

You do know, don't you, that this isn't the life God intended for us? I knew it. That's what the double mind was... and finally

Jesus was able to reach me. He's crafty in all the best ways. Mostly because He's patient and loves so deeply and so strong.

He didn't climb over my walls. He didn't batter at them, causing me to panic and reinforce. He didn't chip away or try to tunnel under. He just sat on the other side. I could hear His muffled comfort as I cried. I could feel the warmth from where He rested with His back against the wall, and it seeped into my bones and something began to thaw. He was just... there.

I took that wall down. I had to get to Him. I needed to be held.

What a sweet surrender it was. That's when Jesus showed me that we are built for friendship. Friendship on purpose, intentional, and deliberate.

I won't lie. I was terrified. Sometimes I still am. But I can do this fellowship thing. Because Jesus showed me how.

Do you know I'm here? Just on the other side. Sitting with my back against the wall, my knees drawn up, my hands clasped together as I pray for you.

I will never coming at your walls with a battering ram. I won't climb over, and won't tunnel under. No chipping away, scout's honor. Can you hear my muffled comfort as you cry? Do you feel the warmth through the stone? When you're ready, I could really use a hug.

How about you?

Dear Lord,

Thank You, most especially, for the one reading this right now. Infuse their spirit with the knowledge of Your love for them, and mine.

In Jesus' Name, Amen...

LET'S GO DEEPER:

1. What kind of walls have you built?

_____

_____

_____

_____

2. How does that make you feel?

_____

_____

_____

_____

3. Write here a verse that helps you to remember that we aren't built to live behind a wall.

_____

_____

_____

_____

4. What is one thing you can do, today, to begin taking your wall down?

_____

_____

_____

_____

WHEN I WALLOW IN MY GROUCH

Is God's comfort too little for you?
Is his gentle word not enough?
(Job 15:11, NLT)

Can I make a confession? Some days I'm a grump. Truly.

I moan and wail and snip at everyone around me. I even get a little undone by attempts to cheer me up. You might say I wallow in my grouch.

I'm really mad at only one person. Me.

I get angry that my body refuses to cooperate. It really makes me fume when I have to miss out on visits and fun and outings. My frustration mounts as I am reminded how weak I have become, and how little I can do. I'm just plain tired of taking my cues from my body. I'm worn out from all the attention my health demands and how quickly it turns against me despite doing my best to take care.

This past weekend I got so aggravated with my own self that I just flat-out told myself, in no uncertain terms, that I was DONE.

Done obeying the demands of my body. Done missing out. Done.

I bet you have been there before.

What always follows a tirade like that is a "pushing" past my body's limits. It isn't pretty and it never ends well. And I'm always left feeling much more miserable than I was to begin with... both physically and emotionally.

I've been studying since this latest episode. I wanted to share with you what I found. I love the verse above.

Is God's comfort too little for you?
Is his gentle word not enough?
(Job 15:11, NLT)

Lord, may it never be!!

Gentle words are a tree of life;
a deceitful tongue crushes the spirit.
(Proverbs 15:4, NLT)

God offers the gentlest of words. The easiest of yokes.

This is what the Lord says—your Redeemer,
the Holy One of Israel:
"I am the Lord your God,
who teaches you what is good for you
and leads you along the paths you should follow.
Oh, that you had listened to my commands!
Then you would have had peace flowing like a gentle river
and righteousness rolling over you like waves in the sea.
(Isaiah 48:17-18, NLT)

I want that peace, Father. I need that peace.

Let my teaching fall on you like rain;
let my speech settle like dew.
Let my words fall like rain on tender grass,
like gentle showers on young plants.
(Deuteronomy 32:2, NLT)

Gentle showers, filling up my parched spirit. Filling up yours.

Because some days, we don't live up to the "overcomer" hype. Some days we just can't imagine that this burden is light. Some days we can only bear the gentle.

As we read these verses together, let's remember that we are to give ourselves no less than we should give each other.

In this new life, it doesn't matter if you are a
Jew or a Gentile, circumcised or uncircumcised,
barbaric, uncivilized, slave, or free. Christ is
all that matters, and he lives in all of us.

Since God chose you to be the holy people he loves, you
must clothe yourselves with tenderhearted mercy, kindness,
humility, gentleness, and patience. Make allowance for
each other's faults, and forgive anyone who offends you.
Remember, the Lord forgave you,
so you must forgive others.
(Colossians 3:11-13, NLT)

Make allowance. Be merciful, kind, gentle, and patient.
Forgive.

Brothers and sisters, we urge you to warn those who are
lazy. Encourage those who are timid. Take tender care of
those who are weak. Be patient with everyone.
(1 Thessalonians 5:14, NLT)

Encourage, take tender care, be patient. With Everyone.
Including yourself.

For examples of patience in suffering, dear brothers and
sisters, look at the prophets who spoke in the name of the
Lord. We give great honor to those who endure under
suffering. For instance, you know about Job, a man of great
endurance. You can see how the Lord was kind to him at
the end, for the Lord is full of tenderness and mercy.
(James 5:10-11, NLT)

The Lord is full of tenderness and mercy. Read the Word and
be encouraged. Then pass that encouragement on.

Finally, all of you should be of one mind. Sympathize with each other. Love each other as brothers and sisters. Be tenderhearted, and keep a humble attitude. Don't repay evil for evil. Don't retaliate with insults when people insult you. Instead, pay them back with a blessing. That is what God has called you to do, and he will grant you his blessing.
(1 Peter 3:8-9, NLT)

Don't be double-minded. You have to live in your body. Sympathize. Love. Be tenderhearted. Don't try to repay or retaliate.

Dear Lord,

Fill me with peace when I'm screaming in anger over my physical situation. Help me to recall the gentleness You offer, and offer the same to myself.

In Jesus' Name, Amen...

LET'S GO DEEPER:

1. What kind of things make it hard for you to treat yourself gently?

_____

_____

_____

_____

2. How would you treat a loved one with the same problem?

_____

_____

_____

_____

3. Write here a verse that helps you to remember that God wants you to be kind to yourself.

_____

_____

_____

_____

4. What is one thing you can do, today, to treat your body with kindness?

_____

_____

_____

_____

DOES JESUS UNDERSTAND?

The Scriptures tell us, "The first man, Adam, became a living person." But the last Adam—that is, Christ—is a life-giving Spirit. What comes first is the natural body, then the spiritual body comes later. Adam, the first man, was made from the dust of the earth, while Christ, the second man, came from heaven. Earthly people are like the earthly man, and heavenly people are like the heavenly man.
Just as we are now like the earthly man,
we will someday be like the heavenly man.
(1 Corinthians 15:45-49, NLT)

How can He possibly know? How can He possibly understand?

There is no way He could "get it". What it feels like to not be able to be a partner to your spouse anymore. How it feels when they put you under to drill into your skull for the second time in as many years. The pain of knowing you will never be able to run and play with your kids again. Ever.

I'm sure each of you can fill in your own blanks. What things are you certain God just doesn't "get"?

Here's the thing, Dear Ones. Lean in, because I don't want you to miss this.

That moment... you know the one... the moment Jesus hung on that cross and made Himself the sacrifice (I mean **the** sacrifice) He took on every sin, every broken promise, every lost soul, every bitter repercussion of that moment in the garden... you know the one... the moment we screwed it all up.

Jesus took on everything from that moment and into all time. He carried it within Himself. He experienced every awful moment, every terrible pain. He grieved each and every loss and accepted all the consequences.

The least of the things our Savior experienced was what it feels like to not be a partner to your spouse anymore. The easiest thing for Him to bear that day was what it feels like when they put you under for brain surgery. He didn't even flinch when He felt what it is to know that you will never be able to run and play with your kids again.

I'm sure you can each fill in your own blanks. Still so certain that God just doesn't "get it"?

We have this beautiful promise, and it's not just words on a page, or platitudes from an absent God.

Read it carefully. Take it in. Trust it is the truth.

So then, since we have a great High Priest who has entered heaven, Jesus the Son of God, let us hold firmly to what we believe.

This High Priest of ours understands our weaknesses, for he faced all of the same testings we do, yet he did not sin. So let us come boldly to the throne of our gracious God. There we will receive his mercy, and we will find grace to help us when we need it most.
(Hebrews 4:14-16, NLT)

Jesus understands. Not just temptations, but each of our individual temptations. Not just pain, but each of our specific pains.

Not just fear, but every particular fear you and I have.

The fall is what brought these things into the world. Christ redeemed it all. He gets it. And He cares. Oh, He cares.

Dear Lord,

Forgive us when we doubt. Forgive us when we fear and cower and wonder. I cannot fathom how or why You would do such a thing for one such as I. I love You.

In Jesus' Name, Amen...

LET'S GO DEEPER:

1. What struggles do you sometimes feel that God might not understand?

_____

_____

_____

_____

2. What makes you feel that way?

_____

_____

_____

_____

3. Write here a verse that reminds you that our Savior understands.

_____

_____

_____

_____

4. What is one thing you can do, today, to begin to feel understood and cared for?

_____

_____

_____

_____

www.ingramcontent.com/pod-product-compliance
Lightning Source LLC
LaVergne TN
LVHW051420080426
835508LV00022B/3175